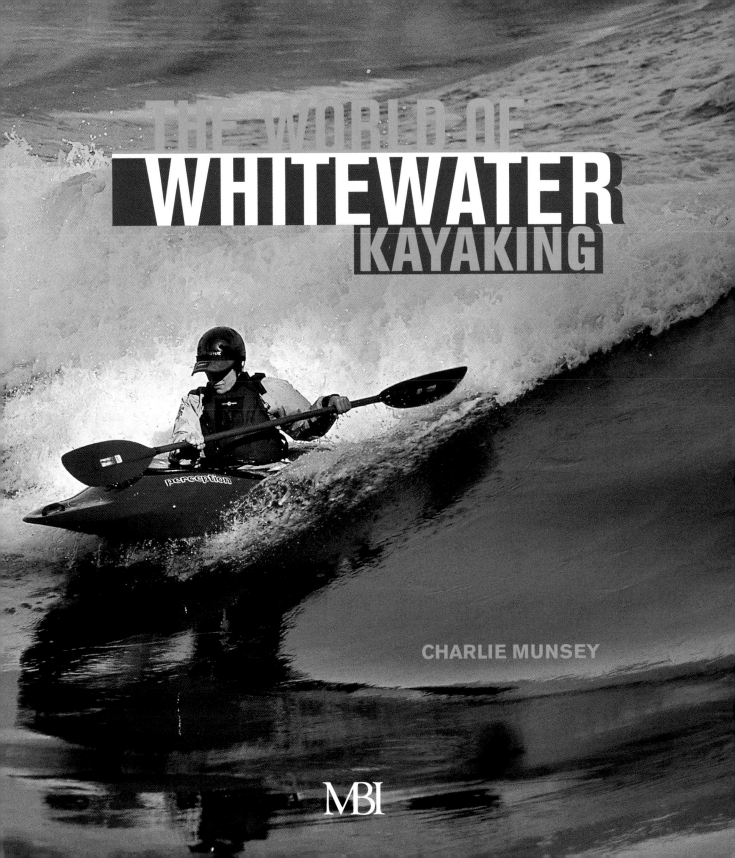

# THE WORLD OF
# WHITEWATER
# KAYAKING

**CHARLIE MUNSEY**

MBI

To my father and best friend,
Charles R. Munsey.
Without his love, guidance, and support, this book
would have never happened.

ISBN 0-7603-1962-6

ON THE FRONT COVER: World-class kayaker and filmmaker Scott Lindgren has a little fun in his backyard: the North Fork of California's American River.

ON THE FRONTISPIECE: Steve Fisher was voted the 2003 World's Best Overall Kayaker. Check him out at www.stevefisher.net.

ON THE TITLE PAGE: Dawn Blancaflor surfs the Skookumchuck Narrows in British Columbia.

ON THE BACK COVER: John Metz and Brett Gleason explore Eagle Creek, Oregon.

Edited by Dennis Pernu and Amy Glaser
Designed by Rochelle Schultz

Printed in Malaysia

# Contents

Trip Jennings on the first descent of Rock Creek Falls in the Cascade Mountains of Washington state.

## ACKNOWLEDGMENTS

There are many people to thank for their help in completing this book, especially the kayakers whom I have had the privilege of paddling with and photographing.

Even more so, I would like to give a special thanks to the wild rivers that have made my journey thus far one that words can't describe . . . only photographs give a glimpse into this world. In the end, I hope they evoke a sense of adventure, yet reconfirm our responsibility to preserve our life-giving rivers.

Kiwi kayaker Ben Brown cruises the Sierra granite toward the
put-in of California's Dinkey Creek.

Charlie Munsey self-portrait, taken on a train from the Susitna
River take-out in Alaska.

# FOREWORD

For almost two decades, Charlie Munsey has been one of the top young expedition kayakers in the world, doing first descents of challenging rivers all over the planet. Starting almost 20 years ago as a talented teenaged kayaker with a hunger for difficult whitewater, he has also dedicated himself to learning the art of outdoor photography, bringing the same quiet, focused intensity to both disciplines. Using both his talents as a world-class adventure athlete and a photographer, he has developed a style all his own, with a focus on action and angles.

Charlie (cmunseyphoto@aol.com) is a veteran of many expeditions to the Himalayas in Nepal and Tibet, as well as to dozens of mountain ranges, canyons, and rivers across North and South America. Beyond the water, he has successfully captured remarkable action images and beautiful scenes of outdoor sports such as climbing and skiing, hiking and running, and canyoneering and mountain biking. Through these ventures, he has developed a keen eye for people and culture, apparent in his portraits of Tibetans in a pilgrimage around sacred Mt. Kailas and of villagers and children in Nepal.

Rivers and water are Charlie's passions. His portfolio literally overflows with amazing photographs capturing all aspects of watersports, from paddle touring and sea kayaking in serene surroundings, to whitewater rafting and extreme kayaking in steep rapids and huge waterfalls. Perhaps the most riveting, however, are his expedition photos, which evoke the experience and inspiration of "big water" expedition kayaking at its best: a small team moving through otherworldly places of immense rapids, sheer rock walls, and rough-hewn landscapes. Many of the photographs are so striking that the viewer doesn't even have to know where they were taken to be transported there. Charlie is drawn to the places that show how small humans are, where rivers carve the earth's bedrock to form magnificent canyons, where cultures measure their age in millennia, and where close friendships make journeys through such places possible.

Charlie has done a remarkable job illustrating the magic of flowing water and unquestionably has become one of the top outdoor adventure photographers in the world, as you will see in the pages of this book. For those who have the great pleasure of knowing him, he is a favorite expedition partner because of his attitude, which is perhaps best summarized by his comment, "The river is my teacher."

*—Doug Ammons, April 2004*

# CHAPTER 1

# What's the Buzz About Kayaking?

ONE OF THE FIRST major river descents to catch the world's attention occurred in 1869, when an expedition led by Major John Wesley Powell made the first run down the Colorado River's Grand Canyon in wooden dories. This expedition would set the bar for whitewater epics, while forever changing the history of river-running. Since Powell's historic expedition, the pursuit of whitewater adventure—especially kayaking—has become extremely popular. After paddling around the world for almost 20 years, I want to share with you how enjoyable and life-changing kayaking can be. This book takes a colorful look at whitewater kayaking, what it's all about, and why it has become a way of life for so many of its participants.

Kayaks differ from canoes in that they have front and rear top decks. The only place water can enter is through the cockpit where the paddler sits in the center of the boat. To prevent this, kayakers wear a specialized spray skirt usually made of neoprene or Kevlar that forms a waterproof seal around their waist and the cockpit rim. This seal gives the boat floatation and keeps it from taking on water. The dimensions of a kayak determine how it will perform. Having the capability to navigate, along with the ability to recover (i.e., roll up after capsizing), makes the kayak an extremely versatile and forgiving craft for running whitewater.

A kayaker pauses after running a slide in the old-growth forest of Oregon's Columbia River Gorge.

In the twenty-first century, the sport of whitewater kayaking has emerged as more than just a buzz. As whitewater guru, Rob Lesser, once said, "Kayaking gives us a way to experience and become a part of the kinetic energy flowing from mountain to sea." Most kayakers will tell you they don't paddle for the adrenaline rush; it's the physical and mental challenges along the way, combined with a love for the outdoors, that makes kayaking special.

Guru and living kayak legend Rob Lesser.

Traditional river craft in Tibet fabricated from yak skins.

## THE SPIRIT OF KAYAKING

Humans have been traveling down rivers since the beginning of our existence. Carved-out trees, which are still used today, were some of the most primitive of those first riverboats. The Arctic people, who spread from the Aleutian Islands to the eastern coast of Greenland, are credited with inventing the kayak. Archaeologists have uncovered evidence that suggests kayaks have been around more than 4,000 years. Constructed with wooden frames, animal skins, oil, and sinew, these early kayaks were very functional and complex.

The word *kayak* means "hunter's boat," and paddle skills including the Eskimo roll were developed and used for survival. Taking a swim (a "wet exit") was simply not an option for these people as they hunted in violent, 37-degree-Fahrenheit seas. Progress has since afforded people the time to recreate, and fortunately, we don't have to face the icy waters of the Arctic for survival. It's these native origins, however, that gave rise to the sport of kayaking, and it's this spirit of adventure that kayaking still offers. As David W. Zimmerly wrote in his book, *Qajaq: Kayaks of Siberia and Alaska*:

The Arctic kayak appeals to us on an emotional level. . . . It has a romantic image associated with fur-clad Eskimos silently gliding along, hunting their sustenance or playing like otters in the waves; it illustrates the artistry and ingenuity of man in fashioning a superior means of transportation in an unforgiving climate. But perhaps we relate to the kayak on an even deeper level—it represents a means of man becoming at one with the rhythms of the sea; and as a means of transportation, it represents a singular image of freedom.

From the day a beginner executes their first combat roll, they're usually hooked. A severe case of "whitewater fever" typically sets in, and the rest is history. Like magic carpets, kayaks can take you places you've only dreamed about. Places that will inspire you. Rock theaters where hidden waterfalls thunder toward the sea and rainbows bounce off canyon walls. Places that teach you about life and where paddlers forge lasting friendships.

From the Himalayas to the Andes, from the Alps to the Sierras, our planet is dripping with rivers. Kayaking offers a way to plug into this dynamic cycle of flowing water. It also provides a ticket to adventure and discovery

Kayaker and downhill skier Danielle Crist greets a remote Nepal village with an Eskimo Roll.

for paddlers at every level. Whether you enjoy the tranquility of paddling through a wildlife refuge or the challenge of hucking a thundering waterfall, whitewater kayaking can take you there. Imagine having the ability to fully immerse yourself in the chaos of turbulent whitewater and emerge unscathed with newly acquired insight and a sense of satisfaction. Let's zoom in on a few aspects of kayaking that paddlers find most rewarding.

Danielle Crist takes in the moment on sacred Lake Phoksumdo in Peter Matthiessen's land of *The Snow Leopard,* Dolpo, Nepal.

Scott Lindgren and Jed Weingarten on a Sierra magic carpet ride. Dinkey Creek, in California, is named after a small dog that met its maker fighting a grizzly near this creek in the 1800s.

## FUN IN THE SUN AND COLD

There's nothing like a hot day on the river kayaking with good friends. Whether it's a simple surf session at the local play wave, a day running waterfalls, or paddling in a remote canyon far away, you're guaranteed exciting and memorable experiences. In general, most paddlers prefer warm water and weather, thus earning the nickname "fair-weather kayakers." Warm conditions mean you don't get

Two of the author's best friends, Dawn Blancaflor and Abraham, enjoy a hot, sunny day together on the river.

an ice cream headache if you roll upside down, and your hands aren't numb and in pain. Many kayakers, however, live in places like Alaska where it doesn't get very warm. They either tough it out and get used to being cold or they buy a Gore-Tex dry suit and other cold-water accessories that buffer the cold. As long as you're warm, you're going to have fun. When your body gets too cold, however, you lose mobility and good judgment. Many diehard kayakers live the entire year under the warm summer sun, spending April through October in the Northern Hemisphere and November through March in the Southern Hemisphere.

## MENTAL AND PHYSICAL CHALLENGES

Meeting physical and psychological challenges is at the heart of kayaking. People with a great fear of water should probably choose another hobby because being upside down in the river is inevitable. Because rolling up is not that hard, it's really no big deal, but complete immersion and occasionally taking a swim are part of the game. Swims and crashes *can* result in serious injury and even death, but they usually bruise only egos and confidence. The physical part of kayaking is challenging and very satisfying in its own right but it's the mental and emotional challenges that accompany the physical part that many paddlers find so rewarding. Setting goals, exploring personal limits, and overcoming adversity are the factors that make kayaking so rewarding and challenging.

Expedition kayaking in the Himalayas on Nepal's Upper Karnali River in 1999.

Legendary paddlers Mick Hopkinson (left) of New Zealand and Mike Jones of the United Kingdom pose at Mt. Everest base camp with kayaks on the historic first descent of Nepal's Dudh Kosi River in 1976. The pair also made a historic first descent of Africa's Upper Blue Nile together in 1972.
*Eric Jones*

## CREATE YOUR OWN ADVENTURE

Whether it is a day trip or a major expedition, kayaking provides real adventure. This is true at every level of the sport. Every kayaker has a learning curve that continues to present new challenges. From the first time you get knocked over to the last rapid you paddle, it's a continuous adventure. Though there are some incredibly talented paddlers, no one has ever completely mastered all the skills of river-running and reading whitewater. Even as we enter the twenty-first century, kayakers are still learning the boundaries of what's possible.

Paddling new rivers and first descents also provide adventure for kayakers. In most river corridors, you'll find that time has stood still, providing a window into the past. Just knowing that a big waterfall lies downstream can be enough to get the butterflies going, as you wonder what's around the next corner. Rivers are everywhere and many guidebooks can point you in the right direction; however finding and pursuing your own challenges is also a lot of fun. Pouring over topographical maps and researching rivers can lead to new discoveries and give you an appreciation for those who have been there before.

## KAYAKING COMES OF AGE

Back in the late 1960s and early 1970s, whitewater kayaking was in its infancy. There was no kayak industry. Boats were made in garages and in backyards around the world. Kayaks were designed and layered up with fiberglass that easily shattered on rocks. Paddles were generally heavy and awkward, while lifejackets were rather large and bulky. Wetsuits of the day were designed for scuba divers, and helmets were often of the hockey or motorcycle variety. Even though the equipment had a long way to go, paddlers didn't know the difference, and some very impressive kayak descents were made. As kayaking evolved, so did the equipment, allowing paddlers to push the envelope and expand the limits of running whitewater.

The basic concepts of the kayak have not changed since its beginnings; however, modern materials have made them stronger, lighter, and more resilient. Furthermore, paddling accessories like dry suits, spray skirts, paddles, and lifejackets or personal floatation

A porter carries a kayak and his baby son on the 2002 *Outside* magazine Tsangpo River Expedition in Tibet.

Professional freestyle kayaker Brian Kirk catches some air at
the Skookumchuck Narrows in British Columbia.

Author Charlie Munsey, in his first year of kayaking, does an ender in an old Perception Mirage kayak on Oregon's McKenzie River. Note the waterskiing jacket! *Eric Evans*

devices (PFDs) have improved exponentially and have afforded kayakers the opportunity to attempt more difficult rivers and rapids, while maintaining a relatively high margin of safety.

Modern kayaking for sport and pleasure really evolved from the discipline of slalom kayaking in Europe during the 1960s. Boats had to be 4 meters or 13.2 feet to race. As a result, most kayaks built in the late 1960s and early 1970s were of this competition length and made of fiberglass. By comparison, most kayaks built nowadays are molded from high-tech plastics or composites and range from 6 to 8 feet long.

Europeans dominated the world of slalom kayak racing for many years, and the sport gained popularity in the eastern United States as well. During the early 1970s, American kayaker Eric Evans ruled the U.S. racing circuit but was unable to win any world titles against the skilled Europeans.

As slalom racing evolved, so did the equipment. The first plastic boat was introduced in 1973 when boat designer Tom Johnson presented his Holoform kayak. Though it wasn't completely indestructible, it was able to withstand the abuse of rocks much better than fiberglass. This opened up a new realm of possibilities for kayakers, especially those interested in running steep, boulder-infested creeks. The next big leap occurred in 1978 when Perception Kayaks founder Bill Masters, along with designer Alan Stancil, manufactured a cross-linked plastic boat called the Quest. Two years later Perception introduced the Mirage, which kayak legend Rob Lesser states, "put Perception on the map in the kayaking world."

Over the last 40 years, technology and experimental refinements have allowed companies to make huge advances and changes in the design and manufacturing of kayaks and whitewater equipment. Kayaking has now evolved into a sport in which manufacturers make boats for every discipline, including general recreation, extreme paddling, freestyle, and racing. Kayaker and industry promoter Woody Calloway of kayak-maker liquidlogic says, "Man, you got to have a quiver. It's kind of like a set of golf clubs!" He's right, if you are really into high performance. It is possible, however, to find one kayak that does everything pretty well.

The mid-1980s to the present has been a revolutionary period in the evolution of kayaking. More than 10 kayak manufacturers have emerged, flooding the market with a variety of designs and theories. The biggest change has occurred in boat dimensions and safety features. Instead of being 12 or 13 feet long and 70 gallons in volume, today's boats are more likely to be 6 to 9 feet long with 40- to 60-gallon capacities. In addition, boats today are designed with large "keyhole" cockpits so a kayaker can easily escape if need be. Older boats had smaller cockpits that often restrained your thighs, making it tougher to escape.

Legendary kayaker Walt Blackadar on the Susitna River in Alaska. *Rob Lesser*

## THE STUFF LEGENDS ARE MADE OF

It would be nearly impossible to mention all of the kayakers and milestones that have shaped the sport of kayaking. Sue Taft's book, *The River Chasers*, is an encyclopedia-size volume that gives a very thorough account of this subject. In Chapter 5, I will present some kayakers who are pioneers and lifetime paddlers.

This chapter, however, will end by taking a look at a very

Idahoan Wink Jones commits to Turnback Canyon on the Alsek River in 1998.

Kayakers paddle the Alsek River as it approaches Lowell Lake and the Lowell Glacier near the border of British Columbia and the Yukon in Canada. The location is 50 miles above Turnback Canyon, which left a lasting impression on Walt Blackadar.

special kayaker, a big-water pioneer who made a profound impact on the world of kayaking.

In the late 1960s, a doctor named Walt Blackadar invited kayaker Barbara Wright and some friends to his Idaho home for an all-expenses-paid trip down the Salmon River, the "River of No Return." The only catch was that they had to teach him how to kayak. So at age 43, he began a phenomenal kayaking career.

In 1971, Blackadar, then 48, looked in the mirror and realized he wasn't getting any younger. With that in mind, he took out a life insurance policy, wrote his final will, and paddled off alone into the Canadian wilderness on the wild Alsek River. Downstream laid a foreboding, unexplored chasm of whitewater called Turnback Canyon. There are times when we face everything we are and everything we hope to be, and at 49 Walt must have

known that as he headed into Turnback. It was a first descent and perhaps the most dramatic that will ever be done. When he came out at the bottom, he proclaimed, "Heed my words and don't be an ass! It's unrunnable. I'll never go back, not for $50,000, not for all the tea in China." But Walt had run it and changed kayaking forever. Walt's diary would later be published in *Sports Illustrated,* putting whitewater kayaking in the spotlight.

Walt also made a few films that highlight a courageous kayaker's willingness to paddle beyond the edge and into the unknown to face major whitewater challenges. *The Edge,* shot by adventure filmmaker Roger Brown in 1973, shows Blackadar running Lava Falls Rapid in the Colorado River's Grand Canyon. Walt ran the mighty Class 5 rapid over and over (see Chapter 2 for an explanation of American Whitewater's rating system), hamming it up for the camera. Not only did he repeatedly run the rapid, but he also purposely dropped into the largest holes that most boaters tried to avoid. It was simply Walt's style.

In 1976 and 1977, Walt was featured kayaking the big-water challenges of Devil's Canyon on the Susitna River in Alaska. Shooting for *American Sportsman,* Roger Brown once again took to the skies and filmed Blackadar from a helicopter as he attempted the raging rapids with comrades Rob Lesser, Dick Tero, Roger Hazelwood, and Dee Crouch. The footage is stunning and gives viewers a real sense of the commitment and challenges of big-water kayaking. Even to this day, kayaking the Susitna's Devil's Canyon is a true Class 5 wilderness expedition. Grizzly bears, huge rapids, and unforgiving backcountry are all a part of the "big Sue" experience.

Blackadar has often been described as a larger-than-life character, one of those guys who lived in the moment and had an extreme zest for life. He was a doctor, husband, father, minister, and adventurer willing to go where others would not. He trusted his intuitions and showed the world what was possible.

Unfortunately, Blackadar would not see where kayaking was headed in the twenty-first century. In May 1978, Walt paddled his last rapid as he got pinned on a logjam that had formed on the South Fork of Idaho's Payette River. The rapid he drowned in wasn't that difficult, but the consequences of a single mistake proved fatal. Walt always claimed he "wanted to be buried next to the roar." Now he lies in Garden Valley, Idaho, just downstream from the rapid now called "Blackadar Rapid," that took his life. A well-written account of Blackadar's life and kayaking experiences is provided in the book *Never Turn Back* by Ron Watters.

Tren Long, just above Blackadar's Rapid on the South Fork of the Payette River in Idaho, where Walt Blackadar died on a logjam in May 1978.

Nate Elliott works his way through Frustration Falls in Oregon.

# CHAPTER 2

# Rivers Teach Us Many Things: Finding Your Limits

BEFORE WE START talking about hucking waterfalls and surfing glassy waves, it's important to become familiar with the equipment used in whitewater kayaking and how it has evolved over the years. In addition, as the sport has grown, paddlers have attempted to standardize a way of classifying rapids, waterfalls, and sections of river in terms of relative difficulty. While several different rating systems have been proposed, the most recognized method, which has been adopted by American Whitewater (AW), features scales from Class I through Class VI. Sometimes the various rating systems can get confusing because they are subjective in nature. It's really best to look at a rapid and determine its difficulty for yourself. More than once I have trusted someone else's opinion on a rapid instead of scouting it personally, and I ended up having bad runs because the rapids proved more difficult than I expected.

Brett Gleason takes in the natural beauty of Eagle Creek in Oregon's Columbia River Gorge.

Rob Lesser, Doug Ammons, and Reggie Crist (from left) scout a rapid called V-Drive in Canada's mighty Grand Canyon of the Stikine River.

John Grace goes super big on a drop called Final Falls on the Salmon River in Oregon. The river flows off Mt. Hood.

Scott Ligare catches some air on the granite slides
of some classic California whitewater, a tributary to the
American River.

## WHICH KAYAK IS RIGHT FOR YOU?

Over the last four decades, technology and refinements
have led to a variety of whitewater kayak designs. In
the beginning, boats were fabricated with fiberglass at a
length of 13.2 feet to meet slalom-racing standards.
Even though fiberglass is old school, it still has some
advantages over plastic boats. For one, 'glass boats are
incredibly light, often weighing less than 23 pounds,
compared with as much as 40 pounds for plastic kayaks
of the same size. Second, the coefficient of friction
(frictional drag) between water and fiberglass is much
less than with plastic, providing a smooth, fast ride across
the water. Some kayakers have argued that a fiberglass
boat is safer if one should become trapped or pinned
in the river—a 'glass boat is more likely to disintegrate and
fall apart, freeing a person's body, while a plastic boat
is more likely to fold like Tupperware, possibly pinning a
trapped paddler.

The first plastic boats of the late 1970s and early
1980s followed the slalom trend and were molded to a
length of over 12 feet. If you happen to paddle one of
these old cruisers—like the 13-foot Holoform or the 12.5-
foot Perception Mirage—you'll find it quite an experience.
These boats are incredibly fast and stable going downriver
and are good for learning how to roll, practicing paddle
strokes, and acquiring the basic skills for engaging
moving water. In addition, one can be purchased for $100
or less. The downside of these older boats is that they
lack the performance, comfort, and safety features of the
newer boats—they turn like trains compared to the newer
generation of kayaks that measure between 6 and 9 feet.
Occasionally, professional freestyle kayakers paddle short
fiberglass or composite versions of manufactured plastic

designs. Generally, these boats don't last long because of rock damage, but they make up for their lack of durability in their light and fast performance.

If you find whitewater kayaking is for you, though, a plastic boat is definitely where it's happening. Plastic has revolutionized the kayaking industry. It's amazing how much abuse this material can withstand. The strength of plastic was burned in my memory seven times after seeing semi-trucks run over my kayaks through the rearview mirror. (Always make sure you tie or strap your boats down well!) Fortunately, with plastic boats, big dents usually pop out when left in the sun or subjected to heat. Even if a plastic boat is sliced or severely punctured, tar tape, duct tape, or a P-Tex-like drip plastic can usually prevent a breech from leaking, or at least slow the leak down enough to give you time to make it to the take-out.

Walt Blackadar in a 13.2-foot fiberglass kayak. *Rob Lesser*

BOW END

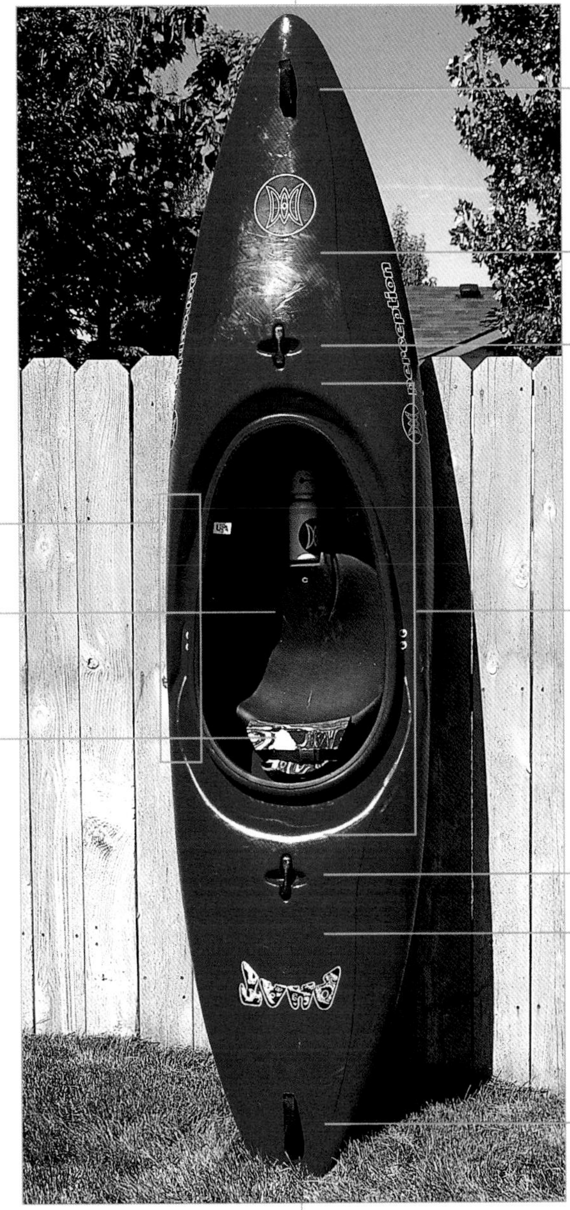

Front grab loop

Front top deck

Front safety loop

Chine (side rails)

Seat

Cockpit area

Backbrace

Rear safety loop

Rear deck

Rear grab loop

STERN END

Dan Givens in one of the early Perception plastic boats that were more than 12 feet long and turned liked trains.

By 1993, the boats were slowly getting shorter. These porters are en route to the Tamur River in eastern Nepal.

In the early 1980s, Perception was the only company making plastic kayaks in the United States. Choosing the brand of kayak you wanted was pretty easy. Since then, more than 10 major companies have emerged, pushing innovation and design in many directions. Each of these companies makes a variety of boats of varying length, shape, and volume distribution designed for different styles of river-running, including steep-creek, big-water, and play boats. There are many great boats made out there—finding the one that you feel most comfortable and confident in is the key. The best way to determine this is to try before you buy. Most new kayaks go for a little more than $1,000, but they will last forever if properly cared for.

## GEAR KIT

A good paddle is essential; damaged or cheap ones can break when you are in the middle of a big rapid, forcing you to swim! Lifejackets are made in a variety of types and sizes. Play boaters like the smaller ones that are lightweight and slim, whereas, river-runners often use higher-buoyancy PFDs with rescue attachments incorporated into the jackets. Helmets are made from plastic, Kevlar, and fiberglass. It's critical that your helmet be padded appropriately and fit snug. A good spray deck is also a key piece of equipment. A badly damaged spray deck will affect the performance of a kayak if it allows too much water to leak in. Before you know it, you'll be up to your neck in whitewater and out of control! River shoes or booties are also essential to have. They protect your feet when you swim and scout, allow you to run on the river bank in times of rescue, and make hiking out of river canyons a heck of a lot easier. You probably don't need them if you're just play-boating but for everything else they're a must.

New Zealander Ben Brown has an E-ticket ride through a
"Disneyland rapid" on the North Fork of Idaho's Payette River
in a playboat.

Ben Brown spends a little downtime in the Taffy Puller on the
North Fork of the Payette River.

Compared to older boats, some of the new play boats are incredibly short. Professional Clay Wright throws down in the Skookumchuck Narrows of British Columbia.

River safety is something many kayakers overlook and are often unprepared for. I recommend every paddler get a copy of the book *River Rescue* by Slim Ray and Les Bechdel. It will give you some ideas of what you can do in river emergency situations. For one, a strong 35- to 70-foot rope can be life saving. Ropes can be used to rescue a swimming kayaker, extract a pinned boat, or haul gear around a portage. Every kayaker has a responsibility to his or her fellow paddling partners to carry a rope. A knife that fits on your lifejacket is also a life-saving tool that paddlers should carry. Knives can be used to release snagged garments or cut ropes that have become entangled or wrapped around people and objects in the river. A few items used in climbing such as pulleys, carabiners, slings, and prussics can also prove invaluable in times of rescue. Many workshops teach river rescue techniques. Generally they inform paddlers on how to work with ropes and tie knots, while also proposing different river rescue techniques and scenarios. Every kayaker should take a river rescue course because river safety isn't all that intuitive, especially in the chaos of an emergency.

Other safety-oriented river items that have grown in popularity include noseplugs, earplugs, and elbow pads for obvious reasons. If you do a lot of play-boating and rolling, then noseplugs are essential. Not everyone needs them, but they sure help in avoiding sinus headaches. Cold water has a way of making ear canals close up, resulting in a condition known as *extosis* or "swimmer's ear." Many coldwater paddlers have started wearing ear plugs to prevent this condition. As steep-creek boating has become more popular with kayakers, so have elbow pads. It's not that funny when a rock outcrop takes a swipe at your funny bone!

Olympic skier and human mountain goat Pete Patterson makes some minor repairs during a six-day expedition in the remote wilds of the Himalayas. He made it out fine—just as he always does!

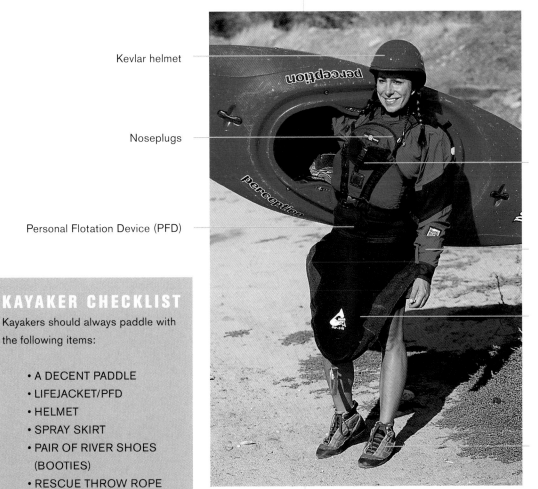

Kevlar helmet

Noseplugs

Personal Flotation Device (PFD)

Place for knife

Gore-Tex
dry top

Neoprene
spraydeck

Proper
footwear

## KAYAKER CHECKLIST

Kayakers should always paddle with
the following items:

- A DECENT PADDLE
- LIFEJACKET/PFD
- HELMET
- SPRAY SKIRT
- PAIR OF RIVER SHOES
  (BOOTIES)
- RESCUE THROW ROPE
- KNIFE
- WHISTLE

Some of these items may cost up to
$150 or more apiece, but when you
really need them, they're worth their
weight in gold.

Doug Ammons checks out the Lowell Glacier, which calves into the Alsek River at Lowell Lake. Don't try this at home, kids!

## DIEHARDS VS. FAIR-WEATHER KAYAKERS

There are two types of paddlers: "diehards" and "fair-weather" kayakers. Diehards are kayakers who are so stoked to be on the river they ignore all negative sensory input, often generated by boating in winter conditions wearing just a thin splash jacket. Fair-weather kayakers, on the other hand, try to stay as comfortable as possible when on the river. By incorporating the right equipment like a dry-top, neoprene gloves, and cap, this can be accomplished. Of course a true fair-weather kayaker only boats on hot, sunny days during the summertime. "Diehard fair-weather" kayakers just follow the sun year round by either alternating between the Northern and Southern hemispheres, or by staying close to the equator.

The truth is that, most kayakers underdress when they paddle. It's easy to do on a hot day, but paddlers should dress according to both the river and the air temperatures. Going down the river bare skin with just a lifejacket in the hot sun feels great, but if you are forced to spend a considerable amount of time immersed in sub-60-degree-Fahrenheit water, you'll soon be in trouble. I have seen this time and again. It can happen if you take a really long swim or if you are forced to spend even 5 to 10 minutes in the water rescuing someone else. Once your body temperature starts dropping and hypothermia becomes a factor, physical stamina and mental faculties dwindle quickly. So, it's always better to overdress because if you get too warm you can just roll upside down and cool off for a while!

Old-school kayaker Don Banducci, founder of Yakima Rack Systems, is fully prepared for the second descent of Turnback Canyon on the Alsek River in 1980. *Rob Lesser*

Brett Valle takes on "Skyscraper," a rapid on the South Fork
of the American River in the California Sierras.

Al Gregory enters a long section of teacup waterfalls
and slides on a tributary of the Tuolomne River in California.
Notice how other kayakers are set up downstream as a
safety precaution.

Fortunately, there are many options when it comes to whitewater accessories. Companies such as Lotus, Patagonia, Kokotat, Teva, and Mountain Surf all make products that will keep you comfortable and prepared for all conditions. A Gore-Tex dry suit, which is a full-body suit with rubber waterproof gaskets around the neck, wrists, and ankles, is just the ticket for cold-weather boating in Alaska or for expedition kayaking, while a shortie splash jacket or neoprene "farmer john" might be perfect for a play paddle session on a hot day in Tennessee.

## THE RATING SYSTEM

Before we discuss the fundamentals of whitewater kayaking, it's important to become familiar with American Whitewater's rating system. Just like climbers and skiers, kayakers have attempted to formulate an official rating system for classifying the difficulty of rivers and rapids. The AW's rating system is included in this chapter and is based on a scale from Class I through Class VI. Over the years Class VI rapids have been considered non-runnable, but as the limits of kayaking continue to expand, these rapids are getting paddled. The rating system is a good basic guide for kayakers, but it can also be confusing. The amount of experience a paddler has will inevitably affect how he or she perceives difficulty. A Class 5 kayaker and Class III kayaker will rank a Class IV differently, so the rating system is subjective. The more you paddle, the more you will learn how the rating system applies to you.

This is also a good time to comment on whitewater guidebooks because they so heavily incorporate the rating system. Guidebooks are great for logistical information, but you have to be careful on how the author has rated the rivers and rapids. You will find that some authors overrate rivers compared with your experience, while

Kayaking guru Willie "River" Kern enters an unnamed gorge on the first descent of the Upper Karnali River near Tibet in 1999.

Lifelong kayaker Bob Beazley gives the "thumbs down" after
scouting a huge drop on Nepal's Upper Karnali in 1995.

others underrate them. Unfortunately, guidebooks can be misleading; for instance, sometimes a particular stretch of river will be described as a Class 5 run, when in fact it's 10 miles of Class III and IV with one Class 5 that can easily be portaged. This misinformation often scares kayakers away from runs that are well within their abilities. Of course, if the Class 5 rapid can't be portaged and is a must-run, then it's a different story and a guidebook can be very helpful.

The rating system given is from the American Whitewater website (www.americanwhitewater.org). The mission of AW is to conserve and restore America's whitewater resources and to enhance opportunities to enjoy them safely. AW maintains a complete national inventory of whitewater rivers, monitors threats to those rivers, publishes information on river conservation, provides technical advice to local groups, works with government agencies, and takes legal action to prevent river abuse when necessary.

If in doubt, scout! Brett Gleason and John Metz check out Punchbowl Falls in Oregon's Columbia River Gorge.

# OFFICIAL AMERICAN WHITEWATER RATING SYSTEM

### CLASS I

EASY. Fast-moving water with riffles and small waves. Few obstructions; all obvious and easily missed with little training. Risk to swimmers is slight; self-rescue is easy.

### CLASS II

NOVICE. Straightforward rapids with wide, clear channels that are evident without scouting. Occasional maneuvering may be required, but rocks and medium-sized waves are easily missed by trained paddlers. Swimmers are seldom injured and group assistance, while helpful, is seldom needed. Rapids that are at the upper end of this difficulty range are designated Class II+.

### CLASS III

INTERMEDIATE. Rapids with moderate, irregular waves, which may be difficult to avoid and which can swamp an open canoe. Complex maneuvers in fast currents and good boat control in tight passages or around ledges are often required; large waves or strainers may be present but are easily avoided. Strong eddies and powerful current effects can be found, particularly on large-volume rivers. Scouting is advisable for inexperienced parties. Injuries while swimming are rare; self-rescue is usually easy, but group assistance may be required to avoid long swims. Rapids that are at the lower or upper end of this difficulty range are designated Class III- or Class III+ respectively.

### CLASS IV

ADVANCED. Intense, powerful but predictable rapids requiring precise boat handling in turbulent water. Depending on the character of the river, it may feature large, unavoidable waves and holes or constricted passages demanding fast maneuvers under pressure. A fast, reliable eddy turn may be needed to initiate maneuvers, scout rapids, or rest. Rapids may require "must" moves above dangerous hazards. Scouting may be necessary the first time down. Risk of injury to swimmers is moderate to high, and water conditions may make self-rescue difficult. Group assistance for rescue is often essential but requires practiced skills. A strong Eskimo roll is highly recommended. Rapids that are at the upper end of this difficulty range are designated Class IV- or Class IV+, respectively.

### CLASS 5

EXPERT. Extremely long, obstructed, or very violent rapids that expose a paddler to added risk. Drops may contain large, unavoidable waves and holes or steep, congested chutes with complex, demanding routes. Rapids may continue for long distances between pools, demanding a high level of fitness. The eddies that exist may be small, turbulent, or difficult to reach. At the high end of the scale, several of these factors may be combined. Scouting is recommended but may be difficult. Swims are dangerous, and rescue is often difficult even for experts. A very reliable Eskimo roll, proper equipment, extensive experience, and practiced rescue skills are essential. Because of the large range of difficulty that exists beyond Class IV, Class 5 is an open-ended, multiple level scale designated by Class 5.0, 5.1, 5.2, and so on. Each of these levels is an order of magnitude more difficult than the last. Example: increasing difficulty from Class 5.0 to Class 5.1 is a similar order of magnitude as increasing from Class IV to Class 5.0.

### CLASS VI:

EXTREME AND EXPLORATORY. These runs have almost never been attempted and often exemplify the extremes of difficulty, unpredictability, and danger. The consequences of errors are very severe and rescue may be impossible. For teams of experts only, at favorable water levels; after close personal inspection and taking all precautions. After a Class VI rapid has been run many times, it's rating may be changed to an appropriate Class 5.x rating.

# CHAPTER 3

# Kayaking Is for All Walks of Life

THROUGH THE MEDIA, kayaking is often portrayed as an extreme sport for daredevils and lunatics! Kayak documentaries usually show paddlers running huge waterfalls or complex rapids where a mistake seems fatal. Like snowskiing, kayaking offers the extreme, but it has something to offer for everyone. I have seen 8-year-olds break out of eddies in Idaho and 80-year-olds, like Donald Bean of the United Kingdom, on wild Himalayan rivers.

Kayaking is a relatively safe sport; the river is usually pretty forgiving when mistakes are made, and it can be argued that the most dangerous aspect of kayaking is traveling to and from the river. Of course, some risk is involved, and over the years rivers have claimed the lives of both beginner and the very best paddlers. They have paid the ultimate price for all of us and should be a constant reminder of how important it is to always be totally alert on the river, paddle as a team, know your limits, and give the river all the respect it deserves.

I highly recommend learning basic whitewater skills and river safety from a qualified instructor or kayak school before you venture out for the first time. Many Class 5 kayakers have never taken a lesson; however, good instruction will keep you from developing bad habits and educate you about river-running as a whole. If you go online or look in some of the major outdoor magazines, you will find outfitters that offer kayak instruction all over the world. There are also a lot of instructional books and videos that give tips on basic skills, play-boating moves, and advanced river-running techniques such as slalom and running waterfalls.

Kayaker Taylor Robertson throws his paddle on Rattlesnake Falls, located on the North Fork of California's American River. The two previous paddlers had broken their paddles across their chests.

## I CAN'T BREATHE! The Wet Exit

It's not a bad idea to learn the wet exit in a swimming pool or lake before taking lessons on the river. The wet exit is the term used when a paddler is forced to exit or swim out of his or her kayak. This happens for a number of reasons, including bad rolling technique, a dislocated shoulder, boat entrapment, and a lost or broken paddle. When a paddler decides to perform a wet exit, he or she first pulls the tab on the spray deck. This breeches the waterproof seal with the cockpit rim and allows water to rush into the kayak. The oxygen-depleted paddler exits the kayak and swims through what lies downstream.

Swimming out of your boat is a big part of kayaking and will always be a possibility as you challenge yourself. Different theories exist on the best way to swim through a rapid. If you swim in a Class I to III rapid, you will probably be able to rescue yourself and your equipment by grabbing your boat and swimming to shore. If you swim in a Class IV to Class VI rapid, you will need to be prepared to take a bit of a beating. You want to protect your head if you're floating into a rock garden, but if at all possible, it's best to "Mark Spitz it" (breaststroke works best) for the shore and forget about your gear. Let your paddling partners retrieve it while you walk downstream to regroup. Wet exits usually result in bruised egos and lessons well taken. (There's a reason for the saying that "All kayakers are between swims.")

The ultimate shuttle vehicle. Although helicopters can make logistics much easier, many regard them as the most dangerous part of any expedition. Doug Ammons, Wink Jones, and Reggie Crist prepare to board a helicopter just below Turnback Canyon on the Alsek River in British Columbia.

Sometimes you gotta pay to play. John Metz hikes his boat up Eagle Creek in Oregon's Columbia River Gorge in search of some quality waterfalls.

Gerry Moffatt films from a "heli" while flying through Turnback Canyon on the Alsek. Helicopters are great for scouting first descents and unknown river corridors.

Watch out behind you! An ox team shuttles kayaks to a river in Chile.

Fresh, crisp air. Bob Beazley and Shane Benedict prepare for the first American kayak descent (third overall) of Nepal's Humla Karnali River in 1995.

## EXECUTING THAT FIRST ROLL

Rolls are what make a kayak the ultimate river craft because they give a kayaker the ability to recover after being knocked upside down (capsizing). It is well worth the time practicing rolls until they are retained in body memory. As with the wet exit, it's best to first practice rolls in a pool before heading out on the river. The physical part of rolling is not the greatest challenge;

Steve Fisher, Dale Jardine, and Ben Brown (from left) scout a drop called Skyscraper on a tributary of California's American River.

rather, keeping your head calm as you execute the roll in a swirl of bubbles is what matters most. There are several types of rolls including the Sweep Roll, C to C, and the Front and Back Deck Roll. All require a sequence of motions that combine a well-executed paddle stroke with a coordinated snap of the hips. If all steps are followed correctly, a kayaker can recover within seconds. Visualizing the steps of the roll is key to learning it. This, along with a good diving mask, will enhance your presence of mind, which tends to be tweaked when you are upside down without air! The Eskimo roll is also a great crowd-pleaser and often awes bystanders watching from the bank.

Regardless of how many rolls you do in a swimming pool, the first one you do on the river, when it counts, will be both overwhelming and special. It's something that you will most likely never forget. This event builds confidence and instills a sense of freedom in kayakers because they realize they have the power to recover when capsized. Performing a good roll allows you to practice new concepts and moves without swimming every time you make a mistake. A good roll also keeps experts from swimming life-threatening rapids when running the extreme. Getting knocked over is all part of the game, so make sure your roll is bomb-proof!

As you continue to perfect the Eskimo roll, you'll soon learn the basic whitewater skills you will need to boat safely and with confidence. Learning to ferry across the river, bracing off the water, catching eddies, surfing, and paddling with good technique are all skills that every beginner should learn. Being able to execute these skills enables one to enjoy almost any Class I to Class III river trip. These skills must be practiced a lot, however, for those who want to take kayaking to the next level: Classes IV through VI.

## READING WHITEWATER: No Two Rapids Are Identical

Even though no two rapids quite look the same, water has a tendency to behave in a fairly predictable manner as it tumbles towards the sea. Understanding this is the very essence of the art and science of reading whitewater. Darwin's rules apply when it comes to a kayaker's ability to successfully read whitewater and execute a safe route through a rapid. What do I mean by "read whitewater"? Like most liquids and gases, water molecules form slabs of flowing water, which create water features like eddies, hydraulics, and subtle currents that are recognizable, readable, and predictable. For example, a hydraulic (hole) is formed when water flows over a rock or shelf in the riverbed. Some hydraulics are safe and provide for great play-boating, while others can be deadly. The nature of a hydraulic allows kayakers to surf and to throw big air moves because it creates buoyancy and keeps them from getting flushed downstream.

The nature of a hydraulic works against you, however, if you run a hard rapid and get stuck in a big keeper hole. You don't have to take kayaking to this level, but if you do, you'll find what you're looking for if you're not careful! I certainly did. One time in 1987 I spent five minutes stuck in a gigantic river-wide hole that could have surfed a house. I did cartwheels, rolls, and loops as giant logs passed by on that rainy November day in Oregon. Just when I thought my life was over, I somehow flushed out downstream.

Some of the most dangerous types of hydraulics are the manmade concrete ones often found near dams, spillways, and old mining/power generator sites. These drops often look relatively straightforward and easy, but they can be deadly. Because they create such uniform

Team W prepares a power breakfast before kayaking the Kaweah River in California.

Gerry Moffatt and Wink Jones in Entry Falls,
big-water boating in the Grand Canyon of British
Columbia's Stikine River.

## WORDS OF WISDOM

Scout Motto No. 1: If in doubt, get out and scout!
Scout Motto No. 2: As William Neely put it, "If you think you're going
to die, you probably will." (Meaning you should portage.)

Two of the sport's greats, Scott Lindgren and Dustin Knapp, on Outside magazine's 2002 first descent of the Tsangpo Gorge.

Gerry Moffatt, from Edinburgh, Scotland, takes a crushing welcome from Wicked Wanda in the Grand Canyon of the Stikine River.

Olympic downhill skier and kayaker Reggie Crist descends the Namche Steps of the legendary Dudh Kosi, Nepal's River of Everest, in 2000.

holes, they have relatively large back-tows that suck and hold anything buoyant. Kayakers, kayaks, swimmers, logs, tires, animals, and more all have a hard time escaping the grip of these features that can turn deadly for a swimmer. Walk around these types of features.

Reading whitewater and scouting rapids can be done from the shore or from a kayak (boat scouting). The former gives you a better look and a more comprehensive view of the rapid because you are higher than the water and can see all the clean lines and obstacles. Sometimes it's difficult to have a clear enough view from your boat. When this happens, you should get out and scout. Scouting will give you the insight on where to go in the rapid or whether to portage and walk around it.

## IT ALL COMES DOWN TO VOLUME AND GRADIENT

Most river guidebooks provide a load of information about the rivers they cover. Probably the most important information listed in any guidebook, however, is the volume and gradient of the river and specifically how it breaks down per mile in terms of its gradient loss. This can also be calculated with good topographic maps and elevation markers or laser-measuring systems. Volume has traditionally been measured in cubic feet per second (cfs) or cubic meters per second (cms). For example, 100 cms is roughly the same as 3,200 cfs. Gradient or elevation loss, on the other hand, is typically measured in terms of feet per mile (fpm). These two factors can tell you a lot about a river and its difficulty.

Extreme kayaker Shannon Carroll "gives her" on the North Fork of the American River in California.

## BIG-WATER BOATING

Big-water or large-volume rivers are typically not very steep and are often referred to as "continuous" in nature. It is a fortunate phenomenon because as a big river approaches an average gradient of more than 50 to 70 fpm, it becomes Class 5 or VI in nature. Big rivers often flow between 10,000 and 200,000 cfs and create gigantic waves, exploding holes, huge whirlpools, and a wild ride. For example, when the Colorado River passes through the Grand Canyon in Arizona, it usually flows between 15,000 cfs and 100,000 cfs. Fortunately for rafters, it only has an average gradient of around 8 fpm. Kayaking through the Grand Canyon is considered a Class III+ or Class IV run. If the average gradient was higher, like 150 fpm, it would be off the scale and most of the rapids would be unrunnable. You probably wouldn't want to go near the place because the ground would be shaking as giant boulders rolled along the river bottom! Before any dams were in place, the Colorado River experienced high flows of more than 500,000 cfs. I highly doubt Walt Blackadar would have run Lava Falls even once at such historic flows.

Extreme kayaker Shannon Carroll.

South African kayaker Dale Jardine enjoys the perfect river on a perfect day in the California's Sierras.

Most runnable big water rivers range from 8,000 to 100,000 cfs with average gradients between 5 and 70 fpm. The major challenge of these types of rivers is dealing with the power of the water. As the volume increases linearly, the power of the water increases exponentially, which is a hard concept to grasp until you feel it. Big-water features such as giant holes can rip you out of your kayak and force you to swim. Sometimes these swims can last for miles and ultimately be fatal. Most of the time, however, a swimmer just ends up drinking a lot of water and feeling like he or she just got out of a washing machine. Some of the most classic big water rivers include the Susitna, Alsek, Stikine, Bio Bio, Futaleufu, the Nile Tributaries, Zambezi, Congo, Tsangpo, and Yangtzee, to name a few.

## STEEP-CREEKING

At the other end of the spectrum are rivers that are steeper in gradient, but generally lower in volume. They are often referred to as "pool drop" in nature. Extreme kayakers descend rivers that drop more than 700 fpm with gradients as low as 150 cfs. These types of steep watersheds are often tributaries of big rivers and provide great waterfall hucking and technical boating. More common numbers for a steep creek would be gradients between 80 and 500 fpm with volumes ranging from 150 to 2,000 cfs.

Charlie Beavers, in his element and right on line! Rogers Creek, British Columbia.

Steep-creeking is more technical than big-water boating. The margin of error is a lot smaller, and there are a lot more rocks to crash into. Serious creekers use short bulbous boats, beefy helmets, and elbow pads for safety. Logjams, low branches, undercut rocks, and pinning are all hazards of steep-creeking. One of the keys to creek boating is to having a "heads up" team that knows how to set up safety measures and work as a fluid unit on the river. Some of the classic kayaking steep creeks in the world can be found in California, British Columbia, Mexico, Chile, Corsica, Norway, and the Alps.

## WATERFALLS

Running waterfalls over 30 feet is a phenomenon that has taken off in the last 15 years. In 1987, British kayaker Shawn Baker ran the 15-meter Sgwe-yr-Eira Falls in Wales and landed in the *Guinness Book of World Records* for the highest waterfall ran in a kayak. Then, in 1998, Tao Berman dropped 98 feet on Johnson Creek Falls outside of Banff, Alberta, to raise the world-record bar another notch. In the summer of 2003, 41-year-old Ed Lucero from New Mexico showed up at the Hay River in the Northwest Territories of Canada and kayaked over an impressive 115-foot drop. At the bottom he was ripped from his boat and held down before he eventually emerged in the pool below. It's unclear if Guinness will recognize Lucero's run as a new record because he didn't

Paddler Fred Corriell living the dream on Skookum Creek, British Columbia.

Tommy "Tsunami" Hilleke on a pre-breakfast paddle through Mamquam Falls, British Columbia.

stay in his kayak at the bottom. Just as this book was going to press, David Grove ran Metlako Falls in Oregon's Columbia Gorge. An official measurement has not been made of the falls, but it's been guesstimated between 90 and 100 feet (see Chapter 5). (As of mid-2004, one person had kayaked down the middle of Niagara Falls—though they found the boat torn to shreds, I don't believe they ever found the kayaker.)

Waterfall running should not be taken lightly. There are techniques, such as boofing or melting down, that kayakers must use when running big drops. Landing flat can result in a broken back. You don't just get in a kayak and push off for the horizon line. Waterfalls can be run safely and can be very forgiving, but you just have to find the right ones and know how to read and run them.

Here's what extreme kayaker Tommy "Tsunami" Hilleke thinks about when he's running a big waterfall:

Many rivers fall somewhere between "continuous" and "pool-drop" in nature. Learning the fundamentals of kayaking and the techniques needed for each style makes kayaking even a greater, more satisfying challenge. Remember . . . you don't have to take it to the extreme to have fun in kayaking. You can find personal challenges at every level.

# CHAPTER 4

# What Style Do You Prefer?

THIS CHAPTER LOOKS AT the different disciplines and types of competitions in whitewater kayaking: downriver racing, slalom, freestyle, and the newest venue to emerge, kayak extreme racing. In addition, I'll introduce you to perhaps the most difficult discipline: expedition kayaking, which can be a window into life-changing exploration and adventure.

## DOWNRIVER RACING: Since the Beginning

As I mentioned in Chapter 1, modern kayaking evolved from slalom paddling in Europe. Before discussing slalom kayaking, however, I want to examine downriver racing, a type of competition that has probably been around for thousands of years. I would imagine that over the years, humans raced their log dugouts, makeshift rafts, and yak boats down the local river. Downriver racing is old, but it has now become fairly specialized.

Most whitewater rodeos (kayak competitions) have a downriver-racing event. Basically, the winner is the kayaker with the fastest time from Point A downstream to Point B. Sometimes the race courses are only 1 mile long, while others are 15 miles long, such as the traditional North Fork of the Payette Fast Get-Together, a race in Idaho in which kayakers paddle as fast as they can for 16 miles down continuous Class 5 rapids. The winning time usually takes about 1 1/2 hours and the winner buys a cold beer for everybody else.

Wink Jones and Doug Ammons exit a rapid called The Wall on the Stikine River in British Columbia. The helicopter was filming for *National Geographic Explorer*.

Rob Lesser and friends line up for the North Fork of the Payette River Fast Get-Together, a 16-mile Class 5 downriver race in Idaho. Paddlers launch from the bridge in one-minute intervals.

Internationally, downriver racing is known as wild-water racing and it's actually a world cup sport. In every rapid there is usually a fast line and a slower line, depending on the nature of the currents and obstacles. A good downriver racer is able to find the fastest lines in every rapid and maintain a high rate of speed through the flat sections of water.

## SLALOM KAYAKING: The Roots of Modern Kayaking

Slalom kayaking is very similar to the slalom in snow-skiing, but there are some major differences. A kayaking slalom course is set up by hanging wires across a rapid and then hanging a set of poles (gates) from the wires. The gap between the poles is about 3 feet wide, and

U.K. paddler Mike Jones in a 13.2-foot slalom boat in the Grand Canyon of the Colorado in 1971. Jones was one of the world's top expedition kayakers of his time. He made a huge impact on the kayaking world with his 1976 descent of the Dudh Kosi, the River of Everest in the Khumbu Region of Nepal. The film and the book documentary trip inspired many kayakers and helped publicize Nepal as a destination for river-runners. Mike died tragically two years later while trying to rescue a friend on the Braldu River in the Karakorum Mountains. He was 25. *John Liddell*

the poles hang a foot or so off the water. The challenge is to go between the poles without any part of your body, paddle, or boat touching them. Sometimes you go through these in a downriver direction, while other times you are required to go through gates while paddling upstream. Course setters position 20 to 25 of these gates in the middle of difficult water features, such as boiling eddy lines and tricky-angled waves that make it challenging to get through without touching. This creates a two- to three-minute obstacle course requiring fast, precise maneuvering and tremendous conditioning. Competitors are scored by fastest time, but are given additional penalty seconds for pole touches and missed gates.

One of the true champions of slalom paddling is U.K. kayaker Richard Fox. Over his slalom-racing career in the 1980s and 1990s, he managed to claim five individual and five team world championships. He now offers clinics on slalom technique, one of which I was fortunate enough to sit in on one day in Idaho. What I remember most vividly is that he could tell me how many paddle strokes it would take to run the entire slalom course. While I struggled to remember the sequence of all 25 gates, he was remembering 250 precise paddle strokes. I realized how focused he was and what it takes to be a world-champion kayaker.

Freestyle pioneer Mark Lyle mesmerizes the crowd at the Ocoee Rodeo in Tennessee. Mark has been a longtime kayak designer for Dagger Kayaks.

## FREESTYLE KAYAKING: Changing with Technology

Though kayakers were experimenting with old-school freestyle moves in the 1970s, it wasn't until 1980 that the discipline of "freestyle paddling" started to gain interest. According to Rob Lesser, the first freestyle rodeo was in 1980 on the Salmon River in Stanley, Idaho. Since then freestyle paddling has become a sport almost of its own, with whitewater freestyle rodeos held all over the world.

The elite paddlers spend more than 300 days a year training and are usually funded by multiple sponsors—a long way from what Lesser envisioned 25 years ago.

Freestyle paddling usually occurs on a standing wave created by the river or a hydraulic that is considered friendly. Kayakers surf these waves and holes and perform all types of acrobatic moves like helixes, blunts, and donkey flips. These are moves that involve wild dynamic action, with kayaks flipping end to end while

Kayakers surf it up at the incredible Skookumchuck Narrows of British Columbia. The wave is created a few times a month by the lunar tides and provides one of the best kayaking play spots in the world.

One of the author's best friends, Eric Evans, and some porters are totally lost in Nepal while searching for the Karnali River in 1991.

## FIRST DESCENT OF THE TSANGPO RIVER GORGE IN TIBET, 2002

After 10 years of planning, a team of international kayakers finally received permission to attempt the Tsangpo Gorge in Tibet, possibly the deepest gorge on Earth. What makes this river so challenging is that it drops an amazing 7,000 feet in 150 miles as it falls off the Tibetan Plateau toward India. That is an average gradient of only 50 fpm, but with flows running between 15,000 and 100,000 cfs in an 18,000-foot gorge, the challenge is daunting.

In 1998, a team from *National Geographic* had a tragic ending to a first attempt when one of its members drowned about 18 miles from the start. The team ended the expedition immediately. In 2002, my friend and longtime paddling partner, Scott Lindgren, obtained a permit for the Tsangpo and assembled a dream team of expedition kayakers. In the winter of 2002, I photographed the expedition with the trail support crew. It took the team almost 15 days to complete the historic first descent of the Upper Tsangpo Gorge, one of the last major river gorges in the world to be descended and explored.

Rivers such as the Susitna, Stikine, Middle Fork of the Kings, San Joaquin, Indus, Karnali, and Tsangpo are among the premier Class 5 multi-day expeditions in the world. Each takes years of paddling to prepare for, and the last thing you want to do is find yourself in the middle of one of these foreboding canyons for the wrong reasons. Rivers have a way of bringing to light all types of truths about the world and ourselves. The river really is a wonderful teacher. Like the rocks we see lying under the water, the river has a way of polishing our souls smooth.

The 2002 *Outside* magazine Tsangpo Expedition Team after completing the Upper Tsangpo Gorge.

From this vantage, the kayakers are barely recognizable in the massive Tsangpo River Gorge.

"Keeper of the Play Spot." Dan Menten, seen here catching some Z's near Idaho's Payette River, is dedicated to not letting too much water get away.

spiraling 360 degrees in the air. There are so many moves these days it's hard to keep track of them all, and new ones are constantly being invented. Freestyle is a great physical activity that allows you to get outside, play in the water, and completely immerse yourself in the primal energy of a river. It also hones your skills and prepares you for running difficult whitewater, should you choose to seek that path.

Back in the 1980s, when the boats were bigger in size and volume, the freestyle moves were quite different. Huge pirouetting endos and 360-degree spins used to be the moves of the day. Surfing backwards was very difficult in those longer boats as well. Now, with boats that are much shorter and designed for play-boating, the moves have become a lot more dynamic and diverse. Kayakers can perform moves no one dreamed about 20 years ago.

Squirt-boating has made major contributions to freestyle's development. Squirts boats are squashed, low-volume, fiberglass boats designed to ride low in the water and sometimes plane like a wing completely underwater. The low volume and sharp edges of these boats allow paddlers to execute dynamic moves such as cartwheels, stern squirts, and mystery moves. Jim Snyder and Jesse Whittemore are considered the godfathers and inventors of the squirt boat, which emerged on the scene in the early 1980s. Jim's talented and eccentric brother Jeff has been an instrumental promoter of squirt-boating. He has also pushed the boundaries of what's possible and has proven a real innovator of the sport. So many of the moves and paddle strokes that squirt-boaters did years ago are what we now see in plastic boat freestyle competitions, but have been taken to the next level.

Steve Fisher wins the 2002 Subaru Gorge Games Kayak Extreme Race on Oregon's White Salmon River by staying ahead of fellow pro Eric Jackson. His win earned him $10,000 for the day.

The wonders of expedition paddling. Wink Jones and
Doug Ammons near the Lowell Glacier on the Alsek River
in British Columbia.

The 1998 Grand Canyon of the Stikine Expedition (left to right): Charlie Munsey, Rob Lesser, Doug Ammons, Reggie Crist, Gerry Moffatt, and Wink Jones.

## THE STIKINE EXPERIENCE

The Grand Canyon of the Stikine River in northern British Columbia, Canada, offers everything one could ask for in a serious Class 5 expedition. It's a narrow, spectacular gorge dominated by complex compressional hydrology, resulting in exploding turbulence and some of the most challenging whitewater in the world.

Descending the Stikine Canyon was first attemped in 1981 and was first fully descended in 1985 by Rob Lesser, Lars Holbeck, and Bob McDougall. Since then, only a few teams have ventured into the Stikine's realm. The Stikine has been the touchstone of my kayaking career, as well. My first time through with partner Conrad Fourney was undoubtedly the best journey of my life. If you're serious about difficult expedition boating, the Stikine will deliver everything you've ever dreamed about.

## EXTREME RACING: Top Dog Racing

Extreme kayak races are the newest type of whitewater competitions to emerge in the world of kayaking. They tend to attract the strong and the bold. It doesn't hurt to be young and resilient, either. Extreme races usually consist of kayakers racing down a stretch of river packed with difficult river obstacles, such as big waterfalls and keeper holes. Sometimes racers go individually and are timed while other races have a shotgun start with head-to-head racing. It's common to see paddles clashing and kayakers running waterfalls upside down and backwards. One of the biggest extreme races to date was the 2002 Subaru Gorge Games, which featured a $10,000 purse for the winner of the extreme kayaking competition. The competition was tight, but at the end of the day, South African Steve Fisher walked away with the prize. Fisher is currently considered one of the top five kayakers in the world.

## EXPEDITION PADDLING: Commitment and Complexities

Expedition paddling has a longer history than any of the other disciplines. When the Spanish conquistidors went in search of El Dorado in 1560, they climbed over the Andes and descended the entire length of the Amazon. In North America, John Wesley Powell descended the Grand Canyon of the Colorado River in the mid-1800s. In the last century, German paddlers Herbert Rittlinger and Walter Ferrentz kayaked the main canyons in Europe and even the upper Amazon tributaries in the 1930s. They used foldboats and pulled their feat off in self-contained multi-day style. Amazingly, they paddled rapids up to solid Class IV without lifejackets or helmets.

Kayaking legend Gerry Moffatt commits to Turnback Canyon on the Alsek River, following in the footsteps and spirit of Walt Blackadar and Rob Lesser.

Scott Lindgren in the middle of Powerhouse Rapid on the Stikine River.

Professional kayaker DixieMarie Prickett surfs the the Skookumchuck Narrows in British Columbia.

Professional kayaker, model, and photographer Tanya Shuman throws a huge aerial blunt on the "dries" of the New River in West Virginia. *Above photo by Jimmy Blakeney*

Wink Jones inspects some visitors' tracks on the "Grizzly Highway" near the Alsek.

Personally, I find expedition paddling the real "cream of the crop." It provides a vehicle for adventure in remote and serene corners of the world where time stands still. There are long kayak expeditions to be done at every level of the difficulty scale. Class II and III expedition boating is like backpacking, but much easier, allowing you to cover a lot of miles without bearing the weight of your gear. Ten-day self-support trips are quite possible with dry bags and the right kind of food.

Class 5 expedition kayaking, on the other hand, demands the same type of commitment and challenges that mountaineering holds. Some take as much planning and dedication as climbing Mt. Everest. This style of paddling captures the spirit of adventure that inspired kayakers such as Walt Blackadar, Mike Jones, Rob Lesser, and Scott Lindgren. The remoteness, exposure, and severe consequences of a major mistake always weigh heavily on a major expedition. Keeping it together emotionally, mentally, and physically is always the hardest part. Not knowing what lies around the next corner and dealing with those fears are all part of the experience. In the end, these types of journeys are exponentially satisfying and leave impressions and lessons that last a lifetime.

*"Paddling continually nourishes my soul, just as rain and sunshine nourish the trees and flowers in springtime as they are about to bud. Paddling brings clarity and focus to my mind in an often chaotic environment. But, most importantly, paddling has introduced my soul and I to some of the most amazing other souls on this planet—the friends I have made from paddling are priceless."*
*—DixieMarie Prickett*

*"A lot of what I like most about paddling are the people I meet and the places I see along the way, as well as the challenges that the sport brings to me. I'm drawn to the sense of fluidity. Anyone who has a passion for something, whether it's a musician playing a guitar or an artist creating a painting, when they're doing what they love, nothing else exists. You simply get into this zone. I'm addicted to this feeling. Every aspect of paddling is challenging. You are constantly learning and relearning. Taking your level of paddling to the next level. Keeping positive and not frustrated as you push your limits. You only learn from your mistakes and understanding this can take you to unlimited horizons."*
*—Tanya Shuman*

# CHAPTER 5

# Whitewater Gurus and Lifetime Paddlers

THE WORLD OF KAYAKING is full of inspiring characters who embrace life and kayaking. In fact, it's difficult to pay homage to all of the influential people and great river-runners who have or are currently having a profound impact on the sport of whitewater kayaking. I've been fortunate to count many of these pioneers among personal friends with whom I've done hard expeditions and play-boating sessions alike. Others I never had the privilege of meeting. Nonetheless, all represent the true nature of the core kayaker, one who chooses the river as a teacher and kayaking as a way of life. They all earned their PhDs in whitewater kayaking, and their stories are unique and inspiring.

So far this book has been an objective look at whitewater kayaking. Here, then, is the human element of kayaking and an opportunity for me to recognize and say thank you to some of my best friends with whom I have traveled many river miles, through foreboding gorges, wondering if we were going to make it out. These guys have been mentors and friends who have inspired me to pursue my dreams and make them happen. Those days on the river were and are the best of times, and this book is the product of those river adventures.

Professional kayaker David Grove runs Metlako Falls on Eagle Creek in Oregon. It measures around 90 feet!

## WHAT LEGENDS ARE MADE OF

Walt Blackadar was a doctor in small town Salmon, Idaho. He was a man in tune with nature and its forces, a father who chose adventure as his ultimate escape from routine, a man who chose to take kayaking into places no one, including himself, thought was survivable. Without a doubt, Walt left behind a legacy, approach, and style that changed kayaking forever.

Although I never personally knew Walt, I have spent a lot of time on the rivers that captured his imagination and moved him. In addition, my mentor Rob Lesser spent some river time with Walt. After Walt drowned in 1978, Rob picked up and carried the torch, followed his true sense of passion for kayak exploration, and took the sport to new heights. Living as a guide in Idaho, I shared a lot of water time with Rob on rivers like the North Fork of the Payette, as well as others like the Stikine. Rob would share some of his stories of Walt and the experiences that he lived in magical river canyons all over the world. After hearing these stories at the tender age of 19, I knew that's what I wanted to do in life. Rivers and kayaking remain a great force and source of inspiration for me. The combination of building lifelong friendships and capturing some remarkable river moments on film has made my journey thoroughly satisfying. The following paddlers are guys I have spent many river miles with, all lifelong paddlers who have made great contributions to the sport of kayaking.

Rob Lesser, Walt, and friends on Alaska's Susitna River in 1976. *Rob Lesser*

Kayaking legend Rob Lesser of Boise, Idaho.

# ROB LESSER

*"Since 1969, kayaking has stirred my life, it has been the focus of my energy and who I am."*
*–"Rapid" Rob Lesser*

Everyone has heroes, and one of mine is definitely kayaker/adventurer Rob Lesser, born in Mt. Home, Idaho in 1945.

Lesser has "been there" and "done that" on rivers all over the world, including many first descents. Rob paddled with Blackadar on the Susitna in 1976 and also led the way in figuring out how to kayak Canada's deepest gorge, the mighty Grand Canyon of the Stikine, a 25-mile rock chasm that to this day has been descended by fewer than 30 kayakers. Amazingly, Rob has been through the Stikine Canyon four times, first attempting it 1981, and first making it completely through the canyon in 1985.

Rob also was instrumental in establishing the retail kayaking industry. Back around 1980, there wasn't much of a retail industry—no local kayak shops selling whitewater products. Rob was friends with Bill Masters, who originally founded Perception Kayaks, the first major American kayak manufacturer. Over several conversations and with some good timing, they worked together and kayaking grew. Bill Masters was the president and CEO of Perception Kayaks, while Lesser became Perception's rep west of the Mississippi. Today, more than 1,000 stores worldwide offer a whole array of whitewater products from at least 10 major companies, which have hundreds of sales reps touring the country.

One of Rob's most important contributions to river sports has been his activism, which has included saving rivers from damming, improving water access, and championing water-rights issues. The North Fork of the Payette in Idaho was doomed to be funneled through a pipe to generate power for western cities until Rob and a grass-roots organization stopped the project—for the time being. This river offers 15 miles of some of the most consistently difficult whitewater in the world. It is truly a classic.

Rob Lesser on the North Fork of Idaho's Payette.
*Monte Moravec*

Doug Ammons plays guitar for porters in Dolpo, Nepal.

## DOUG AMMONS

Another great friend and paddler who has taught me a lot about how to approach challenges is Dr. Doug Ammons from Missoula, Montana. A professional editor, father of five, and dedicated husband with three degrees, including a PhD in psychology, he is unquestionably a man with a full plate. Somehow, with all that going on, he has trained hard and accomplished some amazing goals that he has set for himself.

Doug believes kayaking is as much emotional as it is mental and physical, and he approaches every challenge in life with calmness, boldness, and the strength to prevail against odds that most would find audacious. Doug used to only find time to workout after midnight on Montana flat water with winter temperatures well below freezing.

Doug is a student of the river in the same spirit as Blackadar and his good friend Lesser, finding great satisfaction in the same types of expeditions. Doug's natural talent and strength, along with mental clarity, allowed him to accelerate to the sport's highest level in the 1980s. Perhaps one of the greatest kayaking feats of all time was his 1992 solo descent of the Stikine River Canyon.

Doug Ammons on the first descent of the Thule Bheri River in Dolpo, Nepal.

Doug Ammons runs an unnamed rapid on British
Columbia's Stikine River in 1998.

"There's no way you can foresee how much pressure and stress you'll feel, or be prepared for them. It's one thing to go over it in your mind in your living room at home or talk about it with your paddling partners. It's an entirely different matter to put one step in front of the other and actually find yourself staring at Entry Falls, committed to the canyon. Kayaking the Stikine demands self-honesty, commitment, and performance at the highest level in stark, beautiful, and unforgiving surroundings. At this point, you will find the project growing into a much different and more complex psychological entity than a mere difficult river run—and as such it will also become something that is ultimately more personally satisfying."

—Doug Ammons, solo Stikine expedition, 1992

## GERRY MOFFATT

Around the age of 19, I bumped into a Scottish character surfing a wave in the middle of Idaho. He talked funny, but had incredible charisma, great talent in a kayak, and a way of bringing out the best in people. As the years passed, we became best friends and Gerry showed me what was possible in the realm of worldwide expedition paddling.

Gerry Moffatt approaches 3 Goat Rapid on the Stikine River in 1995.

Adventurer, kayaker, and filmmaker Gerry Moffatt of Scotland.

Gerry has traveled to more than 40 countries in the last 25 years, exploring and kayaking some of the greatest rivers on Earth. In 2003, he became the first paddler to kayak all the major river drainages of Nepal, and he continues to develop river eco-tourism in places such as Bhutan, Sikkim, and India. Gerry has an infectious enthusiasm and inspiring personality and has been featured in film documentaries sponsored by *National Geographic Explorer*, the BBC, and Outdoor Life Network's *Adventure Quest*. He currently paddles and skis as much as possible, while pursuing a career in filmmaking in Sun Valley, Idaho. Equator Expeditions, his production company, creates films full of inspiring stories, hilarious comedy, and stunning visuals. Check out Gerry's world at www.equatornepal.com.

Gerry Moffatt runs Spirit Falls on Washington State's White Salmon River.

## SCOTT LINDGREN

Scott Lindgren is one of the premier expedition kayak leaders in the world. His experience running rivers and making first descents around the planet have made for an unparalleled résumé.

I first met Scott when we where raft guiding together on the Payette rivers in Idaho. He had come from a rafting background, but showed a lot of natural talent and the determination to be a great kayaker. Over our nearly 15-year friendship, we have done many first descents and rivers together, especially in the Himalayas. We've struggled together through all types of scenarios, from losing essential river equipment to getting held at machete point by angry, drunk Tibetan tribesman.

Scott is one of the most solid guys I know in every way. He also has big dreams and recently proved it when he led the 2002 first descent of the Tsangpo Expedition. Both *Outside* magazine and Chevy Avalanche were

Scott Lindgren heads to a river in the California Sierras.

Scott Lindgren on the first descent of Tibet's Upper
Karnali Gorge in 1999. Scott was also the leader of the 2002
*Outside* magazine Tsangpo Expedition.

sponsors, making it the highest profile expedition ever.
It was the greatest challenge of Scott's life, and he put
everything on the line to make it happen. It paid off when
his team became the first to kayak the mysterious and
elusive Tsangpo Gorge of Tibet. He ended up on the July
2002 cover of *Outside* magazine next to the headline
"Mission Impossible." Scott also filmed and produced an

award-winning documentary, *Into the Tsangpo*, which
captures this spectacular river expedition.

Lindgren currently is a cinematographer/
videographer and president of SL Productions, a high-
adventure filmmaking company based in the California
Sierras and dedicated to making passionate and inspiring
adventure films. See his work at www.SLproductions.tv.

## HONORABLE MENTIONS

I have met so many incredible people on my journey as a paddler and photographer. To mention something about every one of them would be impossible. Corran Addison, Eric Jackson, and Scott Shipley, for example, also deserve to be recognized for their great contributions to the sport of whitewater kayaking.  When I tried to make a list of the paddlers I have admired and wanted to mention, that list quickly grew to over 200 names . . . well beyond the scope of this book.  To all of you paddlers whom I know, I have really enjoyed our time on the river and I applaud you for making river-running as a way of life.

Great friends of the author, the Brothers Kern (left to right) Chuck, Johnnie, and Willie Kern. Chuck, the oldest, drowned in 1997. He was an incredible paddler and human being and an inspiration to all with whom he crossed paths.

Dustin Knapp is one of the most experienced all-around kayakers in the world. He's a true champion.

Kayaking creates great camaraderie.
Bob Beazley, Shane Benedict, and author
Charlie Munsey on their 12-day
self-supported trip down Western Nepal's
Humla Karnali River in 1995.

Dustin Knapp, seen here on Tenaya
Creek in California, gets the world record
for the most fun you can have in a kayak.
*Jenning Steger*

**Boofing** – A technique for running vertical drops by which the kayaker often lands flat in the pool below. The resulting sound is often an echoing "boof."

**Broached** – Pinned, trapped. Usually occurs when a kayak is pushed up against a rock or log by the flow of the water and the kayaker becomes entrapped in their boat. An immediate wet exit is usually the best response.

**Confluence** – The point where two rivers merge. In all cultures, confluences seem to be places of significant meaning. Hindus and Buddhists often spread the ashes of their loved ones ashes and build temples at confluences. Be wary: there are often many influences at the conflences.

**Eddy** – River feature in which an upstream current forms behind rocks and near the banks of rivers. Kayakers often pull out of the main current into these pool-like features to rest or get out of the river. This is known as "catching an eddy."

**Ferry** – To cross from one side of a river to the other without losing much distance in the downstream direction.

**Hole Riding** – Usually refers to play-boating, unless you're stuck in the middle of gnarly rapid. Also called "side surfing," this happens when kayakers enter hydraulic features that surf them in a variety of positions.

**Hydraulic** – Often an obstacle in the river where water falls back on itself, creating a dynamic re-circulating feature that can grab a kayaker and not let them go. Small hydraulics are often great play spots. Also referred to as holes, keepers, and recircs.

**Sieve** – Usually refers to an obstacle formed by boulders that have fallen into the riverbed. Water flows through and under the rocks, but obviously a kayaker or swimmer cannot. Water can push a person into these slots, creating a potentially fatal situation.

**Strainer** – A potentially lethal obstacle where water flows through a series of branches or wood, but sometimes through manmade features. Water passes through, but the strainer can pin a kayaker while the current continues to push them against the obstacle.

**Surfing** – Just like in the ocean except on a river, where a wave is able to propagate in one place and allow kayakers and sometimes surfers to catch a ride and do all kinds of tricks.

**Undercut** – Normally created by a rock or rock wall, but sometimes a logjam. These are potentially fatal hazards in which the current can grab a kayaker and pin them against the undercut obstacle, making a rescue imperative.

**Vertical Pin** – This usually occurs in a drop or waterfall when the nose of the kayak gets stuck on a rock at the bottom of the river. The force of the river can push a kayaker forward, making an escape difficult or even impossible.